MALCOLM BOYD

Bach

Chorale
Harmonization
and
Instrumental
Counterpoint

KAHN & AVERILL
London

First published in 1999 by

KAHN & AVERILL

9 Harrington Road, London SW7 3ES

Reprinted 2003, 2005

Part One first published in 1967 by Barry & Rockcliffe
Part Two first published in 1967 by Barry & Rockcliffe

British Library cataloguing in publication data
A catalogue record for this book is available from the British Library

ISBN 1 871082 72 2

Printed in Great Britain by
Halstan & Co Ltd, Amersham, Bucks

PREFACE

The two parts of this volume were originally published as separate booklets. Their re-issue under one cover has provided the opportunity to make a few corrections to both text and music examples, but the basic contents remain unchanged. Taken together, they offer a course in musical technique not dissimilar from that which Bach himself taught. According to his son Wilhelm Friedemann, Bach's pupils began their written studies with four-part chorale harmony, first of all providing only the middle parts and then going on to devise the basses as well; they then proceeded to exercises in fugal counterpoint, 'beginning with two-part ones, and so on'.

It would be idle to pretend that by studying the precepts and examples and then working the exercises in this volume the modern student will acquire the same compositional skill that Bach, or even Bach's pupils, possessed; but he or she will almost certainly arrive at a depth of understanding of Bach's music that cannot be gained in any other way.

Malcolm Boyd
Cardiff, 1999

PART ONE

Chorale Harmonization

CONTENTS

INTRODUCTION

The imitation of Bach's chorale harmonizations has for long, and rightly, been considered an instructive part of a musician's general training. Students themselves nearly always find it stimulating to write 'real' music and to be able to match their efforts not against arbitrary textbook examples, but against music by one of the great composers. This applies even to those for whom the exercise remains purely one of imitation, but the more gifted student will find that the restrictions which a given style imposes will stimulate his invention, perhaps even to the extent of entirely original composition, not necessarily in the same style.

The success of the study will depend to a great extent on how well the given style has been assimilated by the student, and indeed it is largely towards this assimilation that the exercise is directed. Too often the imitations fall short of their models not through any lack of innate musicianship on the student's part, but because Bach's methods have been inadequately studied and insufficiently understood. Harmony textbooks are not always helpful here either, and sometimes misleading. It is not enough to know that such-and-such a procedure is sanctioned by Bach; the student (if he is to produce harmony and texture at all resembling Bach's) must have some idea also of how often it occurs, in what contexts, and, if possible, why. In other words, he must be able to distinguish the typical from the exceptional so that he may know what to imitate and what to avoid in his own attempts to reproduce Bach's chorale style.

The present booklet, in attempting to help the student in this way, presupposes some experience in 'traditional' harmony on his part. It assumes also that he knows how and when to modulate and that he is aware of the nature and function of passing notes, suspensions, and appoggiaturas. The writer's intention is to guide the student in his own investigation of the Bach chorales, and to assist him to reproduce Bachian harmony and texture by drawing attention to those features which distinguish Bach's style. It is *not* his intention to present ready-made formulae for writing 'Bach' chorales, and it is most important that the present booklet should be used side by side with a volume of Bach chorales—never as a replacement for it.

In order to encourage and facilitate this kind of study the reader is frequently referred to examples in the '371' chorales by Bach. Numerical references in the text are to Albert Riemenschneider's edition, published by Schirmer/Chappell.[1] Quantitative analyses are based on the chorales in this volume, omitting those which present duplicate harmonizations, of which there are about twenty-four. Another eleven harmonizations have not been considered here, either because they go beyond the normal chorale style in their texture and figuration (see chorales nos. 270 and 283), or because they are unusually long and elaborate (chorales nos. 132 and 205). Also omitted from the analysis is no. 150, both because it is a unique five-part setting and because it is not by Bach. Figures and tables quoted in the booklet are therefore based upon analysis of the remaining 335 chorales, excluding all repeats.

[1] This is the text most commonly used today, in Great Britain at least. Readers with other editions are referred to Appendix on page 40.

MELODIC CHARACTERISTICS OF THE CHORALE

Before beginning to harmonize a chorale (or any other melody for that matter), the student should pause to consider its salient musical characteristics. The term 'chorale' itself need cause no bewilderment; it is more or less synonymous with our 'hymn tune', and both chorales and hymn tunes exist in great variety. There are certain features, however, which serve to distinguish the chorale from other types of hymn tune, and which make the retention of the German term desirable and on the whole more meaningful than our use of the word *Lieder* for German songs. Since melodic features will partly determine the kind of harmony to be used, it will not be out of place to preface our investigation of Bach's chorale harmony with some remarks upon the nature of the chorales themselves.

This is not the place for a history of Lutheran hymnody, and it need not concern us now that some of the attributes we are about to describe were not necessarily characteristic of the chorale before Bach's time. It is worth pointing out, however, that only a few of the melodies which Bach harmonized and used so extensively in his music were actually written by him. Many of the Lutheran hymn tunes can be traced back to the more popular plainsong melodies of pre-Reformation times, and their modality is often still apparent. Others again were adapted from secular origins, or 'stolen from the Devil' as Luther himself would have it. Of these the best known is undoubtedly the so-called 'Passion' chorale, familiar to most English-speaking congregations as 'O sacred head sore wounded'. This famous tune first appeared in a volume of love songs by Hassler, printed in 1601. Still other melodies were specially written in the two centuries following the Reformation, but by Bach's time interest in chorale composition had largely died out. Interest in the reharmonization of the old melodies, however, was never keener.

During the two hundred years which preceded Bach's appointment as cantor at St Thomas's School, Leipzig, the chorale had quite naturally undergone many changes. The most important of these was that it had lost most of the metrical freedom associated with its earliest period in favour of a steady movement in crotchets and minims, with occasional quavers as passing notes. The typical chorale melody as Bach found it proceeded in a regular $\frac{4}{4}$ metre, usually with one syllable to each note; $\frac{3}{4}$ metre is not uncommon, however, and sometimes both $\frac{4}{4}$ and $\frac{3}{4}$ metres are found in the same chorale (see chorale no. 11). The impression of strength and solidity which this steady rhythmic 'tread' conveys is intensified by a melodic line which combines a preponderance of stepwise movement with an insistence on primary intervals (fourths and fifths). The chorales which embody these melodic and rhythmic features accord well with recurrent Lutheran images of God or Christ as a rock, a fortress, a shield—*ein feste Burg*, in fact. Their very style is like a profession of faith.

The melodic characteristics of the chorale should exert their influence on the kind of harmony and texture one chooses to support it. In the first place, one has to ensure that each of the added parts—alto, tenor, and bass —has sufficient notes for the number of syllables sung by the soprano. Ideally the student should be given the words as well, for these too ought to influence his harmonizations as they certainly influenced Bach's. For practical reasons it is perhaps wise not to insist upon this, but the student should always bear in mind that the parts he is writing are intended to be sung, and for the most part with a change of syllable every crotchet.

Secondly, one must recognize that the crotchet tread of the melody will determine the rate of chord change in the harmony. In fact there will usually be a change of chord (or position of the chord) with every crotchet beat; quavers will, in general, be treated as passing notes, and minims will be harmonized with more than one chord. It may be taken as a general principle that repetition of a chord from a weak to a strong beat will halt the pulse of the music, and this rule is not invalidated by certain exceptions which will be described in a later paragraph.

Finally, the student must endeavour in his treatment of the chorale to match melodic strength with harmonic firmness. The method of achieving this will be the subject of a later section, but it is worth pointing out here that the student needs no particularly advanced knowledge of harmony to begin a study of Bach's chorale style. A good grasp of the formation and function of simple triads and of the dominant seventh is all that should be required in the way of harmonic resource; it is a very simple matter to assimilate the supertonic seventh needed at cadences, and idiomatic use of the diminished seventh soon comes with observation and practice. The cadences provide the pillars for the harmonic structure, and it is towards these that our attention should first be directed.

CADENCES

A glance at any Bach chorale will show a number of pause marks placed above certain notes in the melody. These sometimes puzzle the student at first, particularly when he finds that they are by no means always observed in performance. They are, of course, intended merely as a guide to the singers, and indicate the ends of lines in the text in much the same way as do the double bar lines in most English hymnals. A pause at such places will, in fact, be both appropriate and desirable in most cases, and when it comes to harmonizing a chorale we can normally regard the pause marks as indicating cadence points.

It is most instructive to study carefully the cadence points in Bach's harmonizations, and to observe how carefully the modulations are planned and the cadences chosen to produce the utmost variety without impairing the basic strength of the harmony. As we might expect, perfect cadences predominate because they are required to establish modulation. And root position chords are used far more frequently than inversions because they serve to strengthen the harmony at those places where strength is most needed. The extent of this predominance is clearly shown in the following table, which summarizes the findings of an analysis of all the cadences in the '371' chorales:

Cadence	Root position	Inverted	Total	Approximate Percentage
Perfect (V–I)	1,241	211	1,452	73
Imperfect (?–V)	225	190	415	21
Plagal (IV–I)	30	14	44	2
Interrupted (V–VI)	33	nil	33	1·5
Others (including the final cadences of modal chorales)			50	2·5

The insistence on perfect cadences in root position contributes in no small measure to the overall strength of the harmony, and plagal cadences, with their altogether 'softer' effect, are comparatively little used. Imperfect cadences are, of course, indispensable and, since they come to rest on the dominant, in no way detract from the vigour of the harmony. The small proportion (1·5 per cent) of interrupted closes is rather surprising perhaps, and deserves careful notice. In spite of their usefulness for avoiding undesirable full closes in many contexts, they are on the whole foreign to Bach's chorale style. Most of them, though not all, are to be found in one or another of the following contexts:

(a) As a penultimate cadence when the melody would otherwise invite a full close *in the home key*. See nos. 15, 60, 122, 176, 183, 184, 219, 238, and 241.

(b) In a succession of two or three very short lines, where the unvarying use of perfect cadences would tend to break up too much the flow of the music. See chorales nos. 179, 278, 321, and 360.

(c) In very long chorales, where a greater variety of cadential progressions is naturally more desirable. See chorales nos. 214, 215, 241, and 296.

Unless he is quite certain that it would come into one of these three categories, the student should think again before using an interrupted cadence in a 'Bach' chorale.

Still more to be avoided are any cadences demanding the use of the dominant 13th, or what some textbooks refer to as the first inversion of the mediant chord (IIIb). The chord evidently held no attraction for Bach in this context, and cadential progressions like that in example 1 are very rare

Example 1

indeed. Bach's usual practice in such cases is to modulate to the relative minor (in example 1 this would be to E minor); occasionally, however, he will choose to treat the first note of the cadence as a leading note and make an unexpected move to the subdominant, with the leading note proceeding to the fifth of the next chord (see example 2). The progression is not a common one, and occurs in all less than a score of times in the '371'; it is

Example 2

[No. 1]

nevertheless characteristic, and the student might like to experiment with it from time to time.

Our investigations into Bach's cadences show that, except in imperfect cadences, inversions are greatly outnumbered by root position chords. Moreover, when an inverted cadence *is* used it is almost invariably the first of the two chords which is inverted. Inversion of the pause chord itself is *most unusual*; there are only nineteen instances of it in the nineteen hundred cadences analysed. No doubt the reason is, once again, to achieve the maximum harmonic strength. A few of those which are inverted are dominant sevenths, and there is even one diminished seventh (see chorale no. 327), but on the whole the student would be well advised to use only root position for the pause chords.

Another feature of the pause chord is worth stressing here. Its function as a pillar in the harmonic framework of the chorale is further strengthened by making the chord complete—that is to say, including the fifth as well as the root and the third. This is not an invariable rule, but it does apply to more than ninety-five per cent of Bach's cadences, and is therefore one which the student who aims at a typical harmonization might well regard as invariable. Although, as we have already hinted, observation of the pause in performance will depend largely upon the sense of the text, Bach evidently wanted the harmony at such places to sound as sonorous as possible, and chorale no. 100, in which all six pause chords are incomplete (i.e. lacking the fifth of the harmony) is in this respect most unusual indeed.

Some good reason for the omission of the fifth is usually quite evident to the investigator in those cases where Bach has left it out; often it has been done to avoid consecutive fifths.

Filling out the pause chord in this way frequently makes it impossible for the leading note at the cadence to proceed to the tonic, and the student must here unlearn one of the most common of textbook precepts. In such cases, the leading note will usually fall a third (as in examples 1, 3(b), 3(c), 3(d), 7(a), 7(b), and 8(b)), but it is not uncommon for it to rise to the third of the chord which follows, even when a minor key results in the interval of a diminished fourth (see examples 3(a) and 5). Other resolutions of the leading note are also found, but they are not common and need not be shown here. It is important to note that which ever way the leading note proceeds at a cadence, it is quite wrong to insert passing notes between it and the note which follows. For instance, in example 3(c) the student might be tempted to write a passing note between the G sharp and the E in the alto part; this is *never* found in Bach's work.

Suspensions, a feature of Bach's chorale style in general, should seldom be used at the end of a line. As a rule, Bach makes all the parts halt together at the pause chord, and the student who writes to follow Bach's example in this will introduce a suspension at such places only once in about twenty-five cadences, and reserve most of them for the more elaborate treatment of longer chorales. It is perhaps necessary to add that passing notes will be used between the pause chord and the one which follows it only by those who have forgotten that there are words to be sung.

The crotchet rate of chord change should not be relaxed at the cadences until the pause itself is reached. The inexperienced student will often arrive at the dominant chord too soon, especially where there is a minim in the melody immediately before the pause. In such cases the minim should be harmonized with two chords (as in examples 3(a), 3(c), and 3(d)) or with a suspension resolving into the dominant chord (as in example 6(d)).

The chord of the supertonic seventh, especially in its first inversion (II⁷b), is so commonly found as the approach to a perfect cadence in both major and minor keys that the student would be well advised to memorize the progression and to reproduce it on most of the occasions which permit its use. It is most frequently found in the simple form which we see at example 7(a), and always with the seventh itself prepared in the previous chord. Example 1 shows a slightly embroidered version, and some other variants may be observed in example 3. Examples 3(c) and 3(d) show the supertonic seventh in its chromatic form—that is with the third of the chord sharpened (and also the fifth in a minor key). This chromatic form is by no means uncommon in the Bach chorales, although it occurs less frequently than the plain diatonic form. Perhaps its most useful function

Example 3

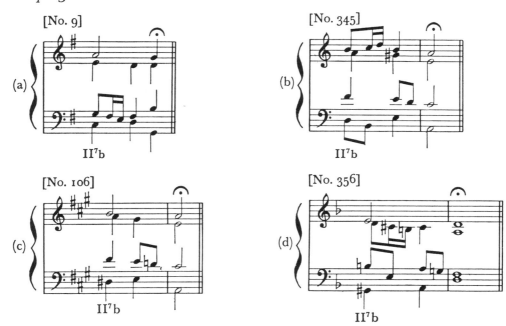

is to avoid exact repetition of a cadence already used earlier in a chorale.

On the subject of cadences there remains to be mentioned only the fact that the final chords of all chorales, including modal and minor ones, are almost invariably major.

HARMONIC RESOURCE

Cadences have been discussed at some length because their proper treatment is absolutely essential for a successful imitation of Bach's style. If the student takes care in preparing the modulations, the cadences, and their approaches, he will find that the rest of the harmony often falls into place with little trouble.

It has already been mentioned that the steady metre and the strong melodic contours of the chorales themselves should be matched in the harmony chosen to support them. This means, in technical terms, placing great reliance on major and minor triads and generally avoiding those chords which produce a 'weaker' effect—particularly diminished triads, and the dominant 7th in root position. Bach's harmony, it is true, goes far beyond these limited resources, but it is wrong to suppose that he used sevenths and chromatic chords in any profusion. Many of us begin with a false idea of Bach's chorale harmony precisely because those of his harmonizations which most readily commend themselves for the emotional response they arouse in us are the least typical. The student will go astray if he attempts to base his chorale style on some of those in the *St Matthew Passion* or on particularly chromatic ones elsewhere (chorale no. 216 for example), no matter how much he may prefer them to more run-of-the-mill harmonizations. Analysis of chorales selected at random from the '371' will soon demonstrate how basically simple Bach's harmony is for the most part. Indeed it is to be recommended that the student should make harmonic analyses of a few chorales before attempting harmonizations of his own. He will probably be astonished to find how far Bach restricts himself to the common major and minor triads. The use of more advanced chords will often be possible, but rarely desirable. The student should aim, therefore, at a strong and fairly simple harmonization, remembering that uncomplicated harmony will give the best chance of achieving the kind of texture that is typical of Bach's style.

Chorales which open with an anacrusis often cause some difficulty when they do not permit the use of V–I harmony over the bar-line. The student who has been correctly taught to change the chord from a weak to a strong beat will go to enormous lengths to avoid opening with two statements of the tonic chord in root position. And yet this is just what Bach does in most cases. In fact, he prefers to open like this even when the melody would permit the use of chords V–I. To repeat a chord over the bar-line is inevitably to rob the first beat of the bar of some of its strength, and it is usually advisable to compensate for this loss of accent, where possible, by writing higher notes in the second chord than in the first. The effect of this in performance will be to make the chord on the strong beat sound louder and more sonorous, and for this reason example 4(a) is to be preferred to example 4(b), although both are by Bach.

Example 4

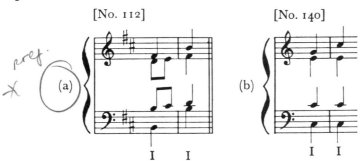

The repetition of a chord from a weak to a strong beat can be applied, in principle, to the beginning of any line of the melody, not necessarily the first. Apart from such places, however, the harmony should continually move forwards towards the next cadence. It is essential, therefore, that the cadences should have been carefully worked out in advance, so that the student (and the listener, even if he is an imaginary being) is quite certain where the harmony is leading. One other point is worth making. Bach rarely used the so-called passing $^6_4$ chord (e.g. I–Vc–Ib, where Vc falls on a weak beat). The only context in which it is at all commonly employed is in the progression IVb–Ic–II⁷b, in both major and minor keys, and the student is advised to reserve it for this progression, preferring VIIb between a tonic triad and its first inversion.

UNESSENTIAL NOTES

While Bach's harmony is basically quite simple in the chorales, his use of
unessential material is always resourceful, and sometimes quite complex.
It is true that some chorale harmonizations (for example nos. 102 and 327)
contain few unessential notes or none at all, but such chorales (most of
them, for some reason, in $\frac{3}{4}$ metre) are not at all typical. The majority make
use of all the possibilities which passing notes and suspensions offer to give
variety and richness to the part-writing, and it is by the texture, as well as
by the harmony itself, that we recognize the distinctive chorale style.

The invigorating effect of accented passing notes should not be overlooked; too often they are forgotten by students who would never miss the
opportunity to use a suspension or an unaccented passing note. The genuine
appoggiatura (an accented dissonance approached by leap), on the other
hand, is entirely foreign to Bach's chorale style. That he was fully aware of
the expressive nature of the appoggiatura is amply demonstrated in other
works where the context demands a yearning or sighing feeling,
but, while such feelings are not entirely foreign to hymn texts, their
expression in appoggiaturas is more in keeping with solo than with choral
settings. The G sharp in the tenor line of example 5 could be regarded
as an appoggiatura resolving into a cadential $\frac{6}{4}$ chord, and a few
progressions like this one do occur in the '371'. Other examples

Example 5

[No. 3]

of appoggiaturas in either melody or added parts are so rare that the student will be wise to leave aside appoggiaturas altogether when imitating the Bach style.

On the whole, Bach follows fairly closely the rule and practice of his day that weak quavers, other than harmony notes, should move by step. Notes of anticipation are fairly common at cadences, but rare elsewhere. The *échappée* is found at cadences, too (see example 6(a)), and the *cambiata* figure is sometimes seen (see example 6(b)), but neither is very common. Other apparent exceptions to the general rule governing quaver movement can often be explained by reference to other parts in the harmony. The opening of chorale no.149, for instance, shows a progression which is by no means unique in Bach's chorale harmonizations (see example 6(c)). It seems at first glance that the soprano C in this example is contravening the

Example 6

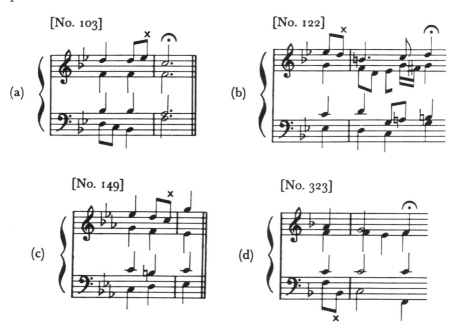

general rule that dissonant quavers should not be quitted by leap, and certainly most textbooks would advise the student to treat the soprano D as an accented passing note. The argument is, of course, that this is just what Bach *has* done. The alto and bass notes in the second chord can be regarded as passing notes and the tenor B as an auxiliary note. This means that the soprano C is, in fact, the only harmony note and its progression by leap therefore quite orthodox.

This might seem a rather laboured defence of a passage which is, after all, quite easy for the ear to accept, and the truth is that Bach himself is unlikely to have thought about it in this way. But it is precisely the absence of any similar explanation which makes the passage shown in example 6(d) far less acceptable to the ear, to the singer, and to the student who aims to write in Bach's style.

CONSECUTIVES

The most interesting and instructive aspect of Bach's treatment of consecutive fifths and octaves in the chorales is not so much the way he uses them as the means he uses to avoid them. He has sometimes been credited with a far less stringent attitude towards consecutives than is the case. The only instance where he regularly permitted himself consecutive fifths was when a note of anticipation at a cadence coincided with the dominant seventh in a lower part (see example 7(a)). Chorale no. 8 shows no less than four such

Example 7

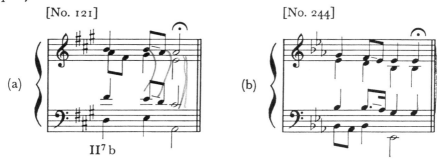

[No. 121]   (a)   II⁷b

[No. 244]   (b)

progressions, although in fact the procedure is far less common than it might have been, and its effect is frequently mollified by delaying the dominant seventh until after the note of anticipation (as in example 7(b)).

There is no truth in the suggestion which some authorities make that Bach was indulgent towards consecutives appearing at the end of one line and the beginning of the next. It is true that a few instances of this are to be found in the '371', and one might mention here chorales nos. 70, 134, 164, 243, 269, 334, and 368. What is sometimes forgotten, or not understood, is that the '371' chorales were taken from cantatas or longer works (including some that are now lost), and that in many of them each line of the chorale was separated from the next by an instrumental passage. When these instrumental passages are removed, as they were for the purpose of inclusion in the '371', consecutives often appear in the vocal parts where, in the original, they do not exist. There can be little doubt that Bach himself would have removed the consecutives if he had intended to perform such chorales as we find them in the '371'.

The strength of the evidence, indeed, suggests that he went to considerable pains to avoid consecutives in such places. Sometimes he did this by omitting the fifth from the pause chord, sometimes by making the parts cross (see example 9(a)), and sometimes by a complete re-arrangement of the voice parts (see chorale no. 297).

Apart from those which occur with anticipatory notes in the soprano and the easily explained occurences between the lines of a chorale, there remain some examples of consecutive fifths which are not easy to account for. But isolated instances (for they are indeed rare) should not tempt us to imitate.a practice of which there is ample evidence to show Bach's disapproval. When we come across consecutives like those in example 8 our first suspicions should be that either the text is at these points corrupt, or that Bach has not spotted the consecutives and would have corrected them if he had.

Example 8

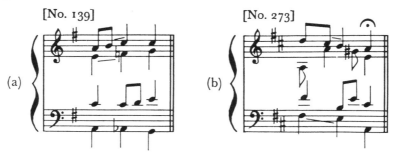

There are, in fact, very few instances of consecutives in the chorales to which an orthodox theoretician would object. Some of Bach's methods of avoiding consecutives, on the other hand, would not always be accepted so readily. Probably the most common of these is the simple expedient of inserting a harmony note into one of the offending parts; the fifths in example 8(b), for instance, are often removed by writing a quaver D between the F sharp and the E in the bass line. Crossing of parts, as has already been mentioned, will often remove unacceptable fifths and octaves— or at least make them acceptable (see example 9)!

Example 9

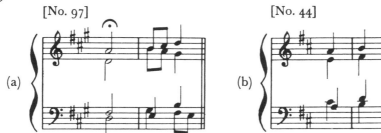

A rather less orthodox method of removing, or avoiding, consecutives is by using a suspension. Bach clearly did not subscribe to the textbook rule that 'any progression which is incorrect without a suspension is incorrect with one'. Nor is there any reason for the student to do so, provided he is quite certain that his practice follows Bach's, which is exemplified in the extracts which follow (see example 10). The suspensions in the first three of these progressions are clearly used to avoid fifths, and the procedure is quite

Example 10

a common one in the chorales. Avoidance of consecutive octaves by the same method, however, is very rare, and the progression shown in example 10(d) is not one which should commend itself to the student.

TEXTURE

Leaving aside those chorales which receive some special treatment (often because they were originally part of a long cantata chorus), it is possible to distinguish three main kinds of texture in Bach's chorale harmonizations. One extreme is a plain setting with few or no unessential notes, examples of which have already been mentioned. The other is a complex proliferation of semiquaver movement, very often in conjunction with a melody somewhat longer than usual (see chorales nos. 132, 197, and 241). The third type, and by far the commonest, is the one towards which the student should first direct his attention. Here the lower parts move mainly in crotchets and quavers, with perhaps occasional semiquavers. Some quaver movement is essential for the typical Bach style, not only to provide interest in the individual voice parts, but also (and perhaps this is just as important) to lend fullness to the sonority.

No matter how many suspensions and passing notes are used, however, the basic texture remains harmonic. Some chorales, it is true, show an interest in contrapuntal possibilities (see chorales nos. 90 and 209), but these are rare and the student should not waste his time trying to introduce imitative phrases into the part-writing. Once the basic harmony has been worked out, beginning with the cadences, his main concern should be for sonority. This involves the use of unessential notes, as we have just stated, and also demands a careful regard for the spacing of the four vocal lines.

The most common error in this respect is to write a tenor part which is too low. Most students, unless corrected, will write for the tenor as though for a first bass voice, in spite of the fact that most tenor voices are comparatively limited in strength and quality below about middle C. Writing in short score, with the bass and tenor sharing the same stave and clef, no doubt aggravates the tendency, and the use of open score has much to commend it. (We know that Bach himself preferred his pupils to use open score for chorales.) A glance at the ledger lines in the printed copy, however, will usually be enough to persuade the student that low tenor lines are uncharacteristic. If not, then let him listen to the tenors soaring upwards in such places as the last line of 'O Lord, who dares to smite Thee?' in the *St Matthew Passion* (chorale no. 50 in the '371').

If Bach appears to lavish particular attention on his tenor lines, there is a good reason for it. The chorale melody itself, because it was designed for congregational use, is necessarily low-pitched as a rule. Consequently the altos must also use the lower part of their range, for to allow the two parts to cross would be to spoil the contours of the chorale melody. Thus the tenor is the only voice which can stand out from the texture without detriment to the given soprano, and the shaping of the tenor part is something which should always exercise the care and imagination of the

student. Although it should not extend above 𝄢 , the tenor should

reach that note and those just below it fairly often. The wide gap between tenor and bass which frequently results does not detract from the sonority, although wide gaps between other parts tend to do so. They may, however, be desirable from time to time in the interests of good part-writing. Crossing of alto and tenor lines is in the Bach style, provided it is done neatly and with audible reason. Tenor and bass lines also cross, but it is important to bear in mind that in such cases Bach always envisioned the doubling of the bass one octave below, either on 16-feet organ stops or in the orchestral basses. Thus the bass part, even when written above the tenor, always remains the true bass of the harmony. On the whole, the student would be well advised to avoid crossing the two lowest parts, at least until he is well familiar with Bach's methods here. Even in Bach's workings it is not very often found.

MODAL CHORALES

It is not often that the student is asked to harmonize a modal chorale, but there are quite a lot of them in the '371' and it is very desirable that he should know something of Bach's methods of dealing with them. It will not be necessary to give a detailed account of the modal system, and those to whom it is unfamiliar need only know that the Dorian, Phrygian, Mixolydian, and Aeolian modes can be represented as extending from D to D, E to E, G to G, and A to A respectively (see example 11). Of these, the first two and the last one are quite commonly found, the most frequent being the Dorian and the least used the Mixolydian.

Example 11

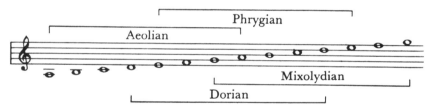

Many of the modal melodies found their way into the Lutheran Church from folksong or from Roman Catholic plainsong, but Bach makes no attempt to treat them in an archaic style. He does not try, in other words, to imitate the harmony of Palestrina or earlier composers. Rather the reverse in fact. Bach treats his modal chorales in such a way as to force them into a tonal system of harmony, at least as far as it is possible to do so. In the case of the Dorian and Aeolian modes this is not difficult, since they closely resemble our D minor and A minor scales, respectively. The problem of recalcitrant notes in the melody is usually solved by adroit modulation. A good example of Bach's methods is chorale no. 110. Here, a Dorian melody has been transposed down one tone, but the key-signature of only two flats cannot disguise the clear feeling of C minor which the harmony conveys.

Modal contours are not always smoothed away as easily as this. Chorale no. 162, for example, appears to begin in D minor and to end in E major (actually the dominant of A minor). The Phrygian mode gives rise to special problems, mainly because of the F natural with which the cadence is approached. In this case, Bach has to be content with an ending which, in terms of major and minor tonality, suggests the dominant chord. To avoid the abrupt and 'unfinished' effect which the Phrygian cadence has upon ears not tuned to modal harmony, he usually draws out the cadence with suspensions—a practice which, as we have observed earlier, he usually avoids elsewhere (see chorales nos. 10, 16, 56, 81, and 352).

The student faced with the task of harmonizing modal chorales will not go far wrong is he treats them tonally (as far as is possible) in accordance with the following observations of Bach's own practice:

Dorian chorales are treated as though in D minor (or its transposed equivalent);

Phrygian chorales are treated as though in A minor (or its transposed equivalent), ending with an imperfect cadence and usually with a suspension:

Mixolydian chorales are treated as though in either G major or C major (or their transposed equivalents). In the latter case, the ending will be 'imperfect' and suspensions will again be desirable;

Aeolian chorales are treated as though in A minor (or its transposed equivalent).

In conclusion, one can only emphasize again the importance of close personal study of the Bach models. Unlike the 48 Preludes and Fugues, the Two-part Inventions, and many of the chorale preludes, they were not written with any didactic intention, and yet they contain an immense amount of valuable instruction for the enquiring mind. If the present survey has in any way helped the reader towards a greater awareness of their value it will have served the sole purpose for which it was written.

EXERCISES

FORKEL tells us that when Bach himself set exercises in chorale harmony for his own students he 'at first set the basses himself and made the pupils invent only the alto and tenor to them. By degrees, he let them also make the basses'. (See H. T. David and A. Mendel, *The Bach Reader* (New York, 1945), p.329.) The practice is one which should commend itself to students today, and particularly to those who, in their 'pre-chorale' training, have perhaps been negligent in their attention towards the spacing and movement of middle parts. Before attempting exercises 1 to 3 the student is advised to read again the remarks on chorale texture on pages 24 to 25; his finished workings should be compared with Bach's own. For those who feel they need more practice than these exercises provide, the 69 chorale melodies with figured bass, included in many editions of Bach's Chorales (Terry's and Riemenschneider's among them), present admirable material.

Exercise 1

No. 9: *Ermuntre dich, mein schwacher Geist*

No. 266: *Herr Jesu Christ, du höchstes Gut*

Exercise 3

No. 121: *Werde munter, mein Gemüte*

In exercises 4 to 14, the student is invited to add all three lower parts, using what he understands by 'normal' chorale harmony and texture. Comparison should again be made with Bach's own workings, and some at least of these exercises should be written in open score.

Exercise 4

No. 101: *Herr Christ, der ein'ge Gott's-Sohn*

Exercise 5

No. 129: *Keinen hat Gott verlassen*

Exercise 6

No. 182: *Wär' Gott nicht mit uns diese Zeit*

30

Exercise 7

No. 24: *Valet will ich dir geben*

Exercise 8

No. 243: *Jesu, du mein liebstes Leben*

Exercise 9

No. 326: *Allein Gott in der Höh' sei Ehr'*

Exercise 10

No. 297: *Jesu, der du meine Seele*

No. 322: *Wenn mein Stündlein vorhanden ist*

Exercise 12

No. 173: *O Herzensangst*

Exercise 13

No. 324: *Jesu, meine Freude*

Exercise 14

No. 260: *Es ist gewisslich an der Zeit*

Exercises 15 to 18 offer modal melodies. Before attempting to harmonize them, students should read again the remarks on Bach's handling of modal chorales (see pages 26 to 27).

Exercise 15

No. 187: *Komm, Gott Schöpfer, heiliger Geist*

Exercise 16

No. 166: *Es stehn vor Gottes Throne*

Exercise 17

No. 208: *Als vierzig Tag' nach Ostern*

Exercise 18

No. 110: *Vater unser im Himmelreich*

For the three chorales which follow the student is invited to provide a more than usually chromatic harmonization. Since they are among the most widely admired of all Bach's chorale harmonizations, he would be well advised to commit the originals to memory. The chorale from which exercise 19 is taken brings to a close the first part of the *St John Passion*, and 21 is the most poignant of many settings of the same tune in the *St Matthew Passion*. Exercise 20 (from the Cantata no. 60, *O Ewigkeit, du Donnerwort*) is remarkable for the 'modern' sound of its harmonies, and was introduced, with Bach's own harmonization, by Alban Berg into the second movement of his Violin Concerto (1935).

Exercise 19

No. 83: *Jesu Leiden, Pein und Tod* (cf. also no. 106)

Exercise 20

No. 216: *Es ist genug; so nimm, Herr*

Exercise 21

No. 89: *O Haupt voll Blut und Wunden*

Finally, four examples in which the treatment goes beyond the normal requirements of chorale style so far as texture is concerned. In these, the style of the opening should be maintained throughout.

Exercise 22
No. 164: *Herr Gott, dich loben alle wir*

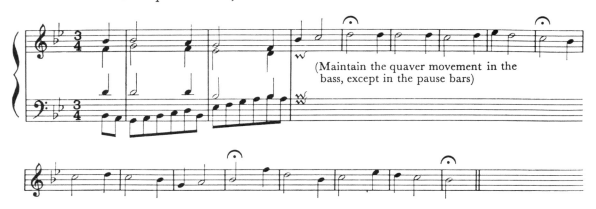

(Maintain the quaver movement in the bass, except in the pause bars)

Exercise 23
No. 331: *Wo soll ich fliehen hin*

[violin]

(Complete the harmonization for S.A.T.B., and the solo violin counterpoint, mostly in quavers)

36

Exercise 24

No. 339: *Wer nur den lieben Gott lässt walten*

(Include a fair amount of semiquaver movement)

Exercise 25

No. 152: *Meinen Jesum lass' ich nicht*

(Maintain the bass quavers, except at cadences)

APPENDIX—INDEX OF CHORALES

The numbering of the chorales mentioned in the text and in the examples of this booklet has followed that in the editions of the *371 Chorales* published by Breitkopf & Härtel and by Schirmer. Those readers with other editions can quickly locate the relevant chorales with the aid of the following index, which relates the numbering in the '371' to that in other publications. Unfortunately, it has not been possible to mention every single volume containing Bach's harmonizations, although it is thought that most of the important ones at present available have been included; those working from editions not here listed will probably have little difficulty in identifying a chorale by means of its title alone.

Figures refer to the numbers of the chorales, except in the case of *Atkins*, where they indicate page numbers, and in the case of *B.-G.*, where they indicate the numbers of volume and pages. Abbreviations are used to distinguish the various editions as follows:

Breitkopf	*371 Vierstimmige Choralgesänge für Klavier oder Orgel oder Harmonium*, by J. S. Bach (Breitkopf & Härtel).
Riemenschneider	*371 Harmonized Chorales and 69 Chorale Melodies with figured bass*, by J. S. Bach, ed. Albert Riemenschneider (Schirmer, 1941).
Terry	*The Four-part Chorales of J. S. Bach*, ed. Charles Sanford Terry (Oxford University Press, 1929; new edition ed. Walter Emery, 1965).
Richter	*389 Choralgesänge für gemischten Chor*, by J. S. Bach, ed. Bernhard Friedrich Richter (Breitkopf & Härtel).
Smend	*Mehrstimmige Choräle*, by J. S. Bach, ed. Ludwig Erk; new and revised edition by Friedrich Smend (Edition Peters, 1932, 2 vols.).
Buszin	*101 Chorales harmonized by J. S. Bach*, ed. Walter E. Buszin (Schmitt, Hall & McCreary, 1952).
Ashby	*The Pianist's Book of Bach Chorales*, 100 Chorales chosen from Terry's complete edition by A. B. Ashby (Oxford University Press).
Atkins	*The Organ Works of J. S. Bach, book XX: The Chorales*, ed. Ivor Atkins (Novello).
Gessner	*60 Selected Four-part Chorales*, by J. S. Bach, ed. A. Gessner (Breitkopf & Härtel, reprinted from *Breitkopf*).
B.-G.	*Bachgesellschaft edition*, except vol. XXXIX (Breitkopf & Härtel).
B.-G. 39	*Choräle für vier Singstimmen aus der Sammlung von C.P.E. Bach*: Bachgesellschaft edition vol. XXXIX, ed. Franz Wüllner (Breitkopf & Härtel, 1892).
L.P.S.	Lea Pocket Scores No. 75. Miniature score edition of *B.-G. 39* (see above).

Breitkopf and Riemenschneider		Terry	Richter	Smend	Buszin	Ashby	Atkins	Gessner	Bachgesellschaft	Bachgesellschaft Vol. XXXIX & L.P.S.
1	Aus meines Herzens Grunde	31	30	30	30	—	—	—	—	17
3	Ach Gott, vom Himmel	8	5	7	—	—	—	3	3²,43	—
8	Freuet euch, ihr Christen	110	105	86	75	28	—	—	7,394	—
9	Ermuntre dich	84	80	69	67	24	—	—	5(ii),59	—
10	Aus tiefer Not schrei' ich	32	31	31	9	9	8	—	7,300	—
11	Jesu, nun sei gepreiset	217	204	157	—	—	—	—	10,58/35,32⁴	—
15	Christ lag in Todesbanden	37	38	—	—	—	14	—	—	25
16	Es woll' uns Gott genädig sein	99	95	84	43	—	—	—	—	58
24	Valet will ich dir geben	324	314	—	—	82	74	24	—	162
27	Es spricht der Unweisen Mund	95	92	81	—	—	—	—	—	55
44	Mach's mit mir, Gott	241	237	—	—	—	—	—	—	124
50	In allen meinen Taten	300	292	230	—	—	—	50	4,164	—
56	Christum wir sollen loben	47	42	44	84	12	16²	—	26,20	—
60	Ich freue mich in dir	186	181	138	—	—	—	60	28,80	—
70	Gott sei gelobet	122	119	95	—	—	—	—	—	69
81	Christus, der uns selig macht	51	49	46	—	14	—	81	12(i),43	—
83	Jesu Leiden, Pein und Tod	206	192	145	—	—	—	—	12(i),39	—
89	O Haupt voll Blut und Wunden	160²	164²	126²	—	—	—	89	4,248²	—
90	Hast du denn, Jesu, dein Angesicht	125	231	179	34³	—	51	—	12(ii),132	—
97	Nun bitten wir den heiligen Geist	262	256	198	—	—	—	—	33,192	—
100	Durch Adams Fall	76²	73²	62²	100²	22²	23²	—	2,252²	—
101	Herr Christ, der ein'ge Gott's-Sohn	132	127	101	—	34	—	—	33,88	—
102	Ermuntre dich	85	81	71	—	—	—	—	10,126	—
103	Nun ruhen alle Wälder	307	295	232	—	—	—	—	2,98	—
106	Jesu Leiden, Pein und Tod	207	193	146	—	—	—	—	12(i),103	—
110	Vater unser im Himmelreich	326	320	249	46	—	75⁴	110	23,66	—
111	Herzliebster Jesu	170	169	130	56	—	—	111	12(i),52	—
112	Wer nur den lieben Gott	381	373	283	—	—	—	112	20(i),98	—
121	Werde munter, mein Gemüte	384	361	287	—	—	—	—	4,173	—
122	Ist Gott mein Schild	197	216	166	—	46	—	—	20(i),118	—
129	Keinen hat Gott verlassen	223	217	167	—	—	—	—	—	116
132	Kyrie, Gott Vater	231	225	—	—	—	52–54⁵	132	—	118
134	Du, o schönes Weltgebäude	75	71	60	—	—	—	134	—	48
139	Warum sollt ich mich denn grämen	348	335	260	—	—	—	139	5(ii),124	—
140	In allen meinen Taten	192	211	162	58	—	—	—	—	114
149	Nicht so traurig, nicht so sehr	261	253	196	—	60	—	—	—	131
150	Welt ade! ich bin dein müde	365	350	274	—	—	—	—	5(i),244	—
162	Das alte Jahr vergangen ist	58	55	51	—	18	19	162	—	35
164	Herr Gott, dich loben alle wir	133	129	—	87	35	—	164	—	73
166	Es stehn vor Gottes Throne	96	93	82	—	—	—	166	—	56
173	O Herzensangst, o Bangigkeit	294	284	—	—	69	—	—	—	147
176	Erstanden ist der heil'ge Christ	88	85	—	—	—	—	—	—	53
179⁶	Wachet auf, ruft uns die Stimme	342	329	256	17	86	82⁷	—	28,284	—
181	Gott hat das Evangelium	120	116	—	—	—	—	—	—	66
182	Wär Gott nicht mit uns	343	330	257	—	—	—	—	2,132	—
183	Nun freut euch, lieben Christen	268	261	202	69	63	—	—	—	135
184	Christ lag in Todesbanden	39⁴	41⁴	39⁴	15⁴	—	—	—	1,124⁴	—
187	Komm, Gott Schöpfer	224	218	168	72	—	49	—	—	117
197	Christ ist erstanden	35/36	36/37	34/35	27	—	13	197	16,214	24
205	Herr Gott, dich loben wir	137	133	—	—	—	—	205	—	75
208	Als vierzig Tag nach Ostern	23	22	—	—	—	—	—	—	14

Breitkopf and Riemenschneider		*Terry*	*Richter*	*Smend*	*Buszin*	*Ashby*	*Atkins*	*Gessner*	*Bachgesellschaft*	*Bachgesellschaft Vol. XXXIX & L.P.S.*
209	Dir, dir, Jehovah	70	67	—	—	21		—	—	46
214	Mitten wir im Leben sind	260	252	—	—	—		214	—	130
215	Verleih uns Frieden gnädiglich	333⁴	321⁴	253⁴	95⁴	—		—	26, 131⁴	—
216	Es ist genug, so nimm, Herr	94	91	80	82	26		—	12(ii), 190	—
219	O wie selig seid ihr doch	311	300	233	—	—		—	—	153
238	Es wird schier der letzte Tag	97	94	83	—	—		238	—	57
241	Was willst du dich	364	349	—	—	92		241	—	172
243	Jesu, du mein liebstes Leben	203	190	—	—	48		—	—	103
244	Jesu, Jesu, du bist mein	204	191	—	—	49		—	—	104
260	Es ist gewisslich an der Zeit	270	262	203	—	64	61¹	—	—	54
266	Herr Jesu Christ, du höchstes Gut	145	144	111	—	—		—	10, 298	—
268	Nun lob mein Seel den Herren	277	269	—	—	66		—	—	136
269	Jesu, der du meine Seele	198	186	142	—	47		—	—	100
270	Befiehl du deine Wege	158	161	121	—	—		270	33, 27	—
273	Ein feste Burg ist unser Gott	79	76	65	—	23		—	18, 378	—
278	Wie schön leuchtet der Morgenstern	392	375	—	—	99		—	—	183
283	Jesu, meine Freude	213	199	150	—	—		—	39, 75	—
294	Herr Jesu Christ, du höchstes Gut	146	142	110	—	—		—	24, 80	—
296	Nun lob mein Seel den Herren	278	270	—	—	—		—	—	137
297	Jesu der du meine Seele	199	188	143	—	—		—	18, 286	—
321	Wir Christenleut	396	379	301	—	—	86	—	7, 377	—
322	Wenn mein Stündlein vorhanden ist	368	353	—	—	—		—	—	175
323	Wie schön leuchtet der Morgenstern	394	376	298	—	—	85⁴	—	35, 69	—
324	Jesu, meine Freude	212	197	152	—	—		—	20(i), 24	—
326	Allein Gott in der Höh sei Ehr	17	13	17	—	5	4	—	23, 116	—
327	Jesu, nun sei gepreiset	218	205	156	—	—		—	37, 257	—
331	Wo soll ich fliehen hin	30	27	26	—	—		—	28, 164	—
334	Für deinen Thron tret ich hiermit	136	132	103	—	—		—	—	74
339	Wer nur den lieben Gott	378	371	280	—	—	84	—	35, 292	—
345	O Haupt voll Blut und Wunden	162	165	127	—	—		345	5(ii), 36	—
352	Es woll' uns Gott genädig sein	98	96	—	—	—		352²	—	59
356	Jesu, meine Freude	208	195	—	—	—		—	—	105
360	Wir Christenleut	395	381	302	—	100		—	5(ii), 126	—
368	Hilf, Herr Jesu, lass gelingen	178	—	311	41	41		—	5(ii), 166	—

¹Minor third lower. ²Tone lower. ³Semitone lower. ⁴Tone higher.
⁵Minor third higher. ⁶Note values halved in *Breitkopf*. ⁷Note values halved.

PART TWO

Instrumental Counterpoint

CONTENTS

INTRODUCTION

Like its companion on the 'Bach' chorales, this booklet has been written in the belief that practice in different aspects of musical style and technique should be preceded and accompanied by a thorough study of the models concerned. Its aim is firstly to guide the student in his study of Bach's two-part and three-part instrumental counterpoint (especially as exemplified in the keyboard suites and Inventions), and secondly to provide exercises whereby he may test his understanding of the techniques involved, and his ability to use them creatively. The intention is not to provide ready-made formulae for putting together pieces in the Bach style—which would be impossible anyway—and the following pages should be regarded only as a method of fruitful study of the works themselves.

In both the text and the musical examples, particular stress has been placed upon the value of the Inventions in two and three parts which Bach wrote at Cöthen towards 1723. Not only do these works provide a useful compendium of Bach's methods elsewhere, but, like many of the other works written at Cöthen, they were expressly designed to instruct. The remarks with which Bach prefaced the 1723 manuscript speak of the Inventions as 'an honest guide to lovers of the keyboard', wherein they might learn 'not only to play clearly in two parts, but also, after further progress, to deal correctly with three *obbligato* parts'. The same preface, however, makes it clear that the composer intended the volume to have an application beyond helping to lay the foundations of good keyboard technique; he intended it also to be used as a means 'to acquire a strong foretaste of composition'. In this way, too, the value of the Inventions to the incipient composer remains undiminished, because the skills they teach have a relevance beyond their own particular forms and style. How to develop musical ideas, how to keep invention alive when inspiration slackens, how to achieve unity in many-voiced textures—these are problems which nearly every composer will face, no matter what personal style of writing he may develop.

The present booklet stops short of the stricter disciplines of canon and fugue but the Inventions themselves provide an admirable introduction to a study of these forms, and in some ways we can look upon them as preliminary essays for the *Well-tempered Clavier* (1722). Like the preludes and fugues in that famous volume, the Inventions are set out in ascending order of keys, although nine of the keys furthest removed from C major are here omitted. Their forms and contrapuntal textures lie somewhere between the comparative freedom of the preludes and the strict organization of the fugues, and the student who has acquired some measure of skill in writing Inventions will be best equipped to deal with the most difficult problem in fugal writing, namely how best to proceed when the mechanics of the exposition can carry the music no further forward.

A study of the Bach Inventions can be profitable even to the student who has no pretensions as a pianist, and whose studies of compositional techniques will never progress beyond fugal expositions. Some knowledge of the Inventions is bound to enhance and deepen his appreciation of Bach's other works, for invention technique lies at the heart of so much of his music—not only keyboard works, such as the 'Forty-eight,' the suites and partitas, but also many movements in the concertos, the cantatas, and the Passions. Besides, they are delightful pieces in their own right.

MELODIC CHARACTERISTICS

Before beginning a study of Bach's contrapuntal technique, it is worth considering the kind of melodies he writes in instrumental works. No matter how clever we might become at combining one part with another, or at devising cunning imitations, canons, augmentations, and so on, we shall never achieve a true Bach sound in our music until we have understood the nature of the individual parts themselves.

Not even his most fervent admirers would claim that Bach was primarily a melodist. We all admire, of course, the beautiful contours of the Lied *Bist du bei mir* and of the Aria 'Schlummert ein' in the church cantata no. 82, *Ich habe genug*, and doubtless every reader will be able to recall other Bach melodies which he prizes highly. Nevertheless, we do not associate Bach with fine melodic writing (by which we usually mean fine *vocal* writing) in the way that we do his contemporary Handel, or other composers such as Mozart, Schubert, Puccini, and Britten. Bach's approach to music was an instrumentalist's, whereas that of the other composers mentioned was in each case predominantly a vocal one. His melodic lines depend not upon lyricism so much as upon the knitting together of short, incisive, and memorable phrases. The opening movement of the third Brandenburg Concerto is a splendid example of how he could compose interesting, vital, and even inspiring music without writing anything which could justly be described as a 'tune'.

In fact the Brandenburg Concertos provide an excellent point of departure for our consideration of Bach's keyboard melody, because the contours of his mature writing for *any* instrument (and often for the voice as well) continually suggest the violin, and this despite the fact that his own reputation was made as an organist. Close contact with instrumental music at Cöthen, where he held the post of Kapellmeister between 1717 and 1723, provided a practical means of perfecting an instrumental style which had already been indicated in the string concertos of Italian composers, especially Albinoni and Vivaldi. His close study of works like these and his experience of orchestral music at Cöthen found expression not only in the Violin Concertos and the Brandenburg Concertos, but also in the keyboard suites and Inventions written at about the same time. The violin concertos, and above all, perhaps, the Concerto in D minor for two violins, are widely considered among the finest examples of the form by any composer, and all violinists would agree that the solo parts are beautifully laid out for the instrument. Yet if we take the trouble to compare the solo lines of the double concerto with the individual parts of the keyboard works a great similarity in style is at once apparent. The quotation from the C minor Partita at example 1(b) has been transposed up a tone to facilitate comparison with the extract from the double concerto shown in example 1(a). Dozens of

Example 1

similar parallels between the string compositions and the keyboard work could be shown.

Bach's violinistic approach in the Inventions and elsewhere results in melodic lines whose dominant characteristic is an unusually high proportion of leaps, including a large number of very wide ones. His tunes do not 'flow' in the sense we usually understand the word, and for this reason singers often complain that the parts he gives to them are difficult and tortuous. Also his melodies are frequently organized in short, and often repetitive, phrases rather than in the long stretches of continuous melody which Handel and other more Italianate composers give us. The 'flow' in Bach's music is of a different kind, and derives mainly from the movement of the harmony implicit in the polyphony or in the melody itself; the importance of the harmony in this respect will be dealt with in a later section. Not all Bach's melodies proceed in wide leaps, of course, and particularly in relaxed moments he can produce melodic lines of predominantly conjunct movement. Nevertheless, since most students seem to associate counterpoint with 'flowing parts', it is important to emphasize the self-evident fact that even in slow movements Bach's instrumental counterpoint is usually of a kind which delights in a leaping, springy melodic line. Those examination questions which invite the candidate to write 'flowing parts in the style of J. S. Bach' are usually self-contradictory.

Melody with a high proportion of leaps will continually imply harmony, as we have already said; but leaps in Bach's music will often imply other things too. It is possible, for instance, for a single line to suggest polyphony, and this helps to explain the extraordinary richness of Bach's counterpoint even when it is written in only two parts. Example 2(a) quotes a passage from the fifth two-part Invention in which a single strand implies the alternation of two voices; in the context of a three-part work the same passage might well have appeared in the way shown at example 2(b), where its implied polyphony has been made explicit.

Example 2

Two-part Invention no. 5, bars 20–23

A melodic figure frequently found in Bach's instrumental writing, and one which again makes use of wide leaps, is of the kind shown at example 3, below. Here two strands are once more implied, but this time only one of them moves, the repeated notes suggesting a stationary pedal. Like so many of Bach's melodic figures, this one too may have had its origin in violin

Example 3

Two-part Invention no. 8, bars 21–22

music, where the bow would alternate between two adjacent strings. Here, though, the passage is obviously just as idiomatic to the keyboard.

Other melodic features of Bach's instrumental style will become apparent during the course of this survey, but even from the few examples so far quoted it will be obvious to the reader that melodic sequences play an important part in the music. Sequence is a device which Bach uses more than any other to extend his melodic phrases and to achieve the formal balance he desires. There is hardly a Bach movement of any length which does not rely heavily upon sequence for its construction; the first of the two-part Inventions, indeed, is almost entirely dependent upon it (see example 13). Like every formal device, however, that of sequence can be overdone, and the student should guard against using it too often or for too long stretches. In particular, he should be ready to jettison it altogether if it threatens to disrupt the harmonic flow. He should also observe that Bach's sequences nearly always move by step in a downwards direction, and that they rarely contain more than three 'limbs', and never more than four. Sequence in one part will usually be matched by sequence in the others (see examples 5(b) and 11), but a change of direction in the final 'limb' can produce a very satisfying effect. A good example of this may be observed in the first two-part Invention at bars 4 and 12.

Most important of all is that the sequence should appear to grow out of the music which precedes it, and that it should never give the impression that a musical phrase has been created merely for the purpose of serving a sequence. From this observation it is possible to formulate the principle that a phrase will not normally be extended in sequence unless it has already been presented in a non-sequential passage.

HARMONY

It may seem odd that a booklet which claims to deal with Bach's counterpoint should begin with sections devoted to his melody and harmony, but in fact the distinction between harmony and counterpoint in Bach's music is a finer one than many would suppose. Melody, harmony, and counterpoint, indeed, are frequently inseparable and interdependent, not only because the melody is constantly implying harmony, but also because the direction of the contrapuntal texture as a whole is determined by the course which the harmony takes through a number of related and well-defined keys. Consideration of the tonal construction of such pieces as the suites and the Inventions will be left for a later section dealing specifically with formal principles, but some consideration of Bach's harmony in general is desirable here, if only to correct a widespread but mistaken belief that harmonic considerations should come last in dealing with Bach's contrapuntal forms.

In fact many good students go wrong in their early attempts to re-create Bach's counterpoint precisely because they devote all their attention to the obvious intricacies of imitation, canon, invertible counterpoint, and so on, and let the harmony take care of itself. This, of course, it will not do, and inevitably the result is a mere succession of notes and phrases with all the appearance of movement and busyness but with absolutely no sense of direction. A sense of direction in Bach's music (particularly when words are not involved) can come only from the harmony, and far better results are likely if the student begins his piece by sketching out the harmonic path which the music will follow. Harmony and counterpoint are inseparable in Bach's music, as we have said, and ideally they should be conceived as one. Until the student can do this, he will find it preferable to make his counterpoint fit the harmony rather than to allow the harmony to fit in with the counterpoint.

A study of chorale harmony can be of immense benefit to the student in this respect, since it focuses his attention upon progressions and sequences of key which provide the basis for instrumental works. No one is likely to produce good Inventions who cannot also reproduce good 'Bach' chorales, because Bach's instrumental counterpoint is often little more than elaboration of chord progressions such as might be found in a chorale. We must add, however, that the harmonic basis of a movement from the keyboard suites or of one of the Inventions is likely to be rather simpler than the harmony found in the average chorale.

It is not always understood that rhythm is largely dependent upon harmony. A change of chord, or even of the position of a chord (i.e. from root position to an inversion or vice versa), produces an accent whose strength depends upon the particular chords involved and their place within the bar. It is possible to write a whole string of quickly reiterated chords and yet produce a slow rhythm, if the chords are changed infrequently. This often happens in the music of Mozart, Beethoven, and other composers of the Classical period, where the harmony may remain the same over a number of bars. This rate of chord change is frequently spoken of as the 'harmonic rhythm' to distinguish it from the melodic rhythm and from the pulse of the music indicated by the time signature. A good grasp of harmonic rhythm is important in writing music of all kinds, but it is often overlooked in contrapuntal studies, where melodic considerations tend to take first place.

In Bach's chorale harmonizations, where the chords (or positions of the chords) usually change with every crotchet, the harmonic rhythm and the $\frac{4}{4}$ time signature coincide. In longer works a much slower rate of chord change is obviously desirable, and the concertos provide many examples of this. The harmonic rhythm of the Inventions, and of other works in invention style, is quicker than in the concertos, but usually slower than in the chorales. The precise rate may vary, and will, in any case, depend to some extent upon the time signature and the speed. In a quick $\frac{3}{8}$ tempo, for example, the harmony might change only once a bar or even two bars, but in the normal $\frac{3}{4}$ or $\frac{4}{4}$ movement the harmonic rhythm usually moves in minims and crotchets.

The student must endeavour to achieve a good sense of harmonic progression and the ability to recognize the harmonic rhythm suitable for the character of the music he is asked to write. Useful practice in cultivating both these abilities may be acquired by reading through the Inventions and other pieces at the keyboard, all the time substituting plain harmonies for Bach's polyphony and where necessary completing the chords which the counterpoint can do no more than suggest. It would be no bad thing either for the student to put his own manuscripts to the same test, discarding or reworking those passages where the counterpoint has produced awkward harmonies or a static harmonic rhythm.

Melodic lines which, like Bach's, are characterized by frequent leaps demand considerable care when they are combined with other parts. Even the best student sometimes finds it difficult to reconcile melodic shape with harmonic propriety and it is well to be clear about Bach's use of unessential notes and suspensions. In general he subscribes to the textbook rule that unessential notes (i.e. notes *not* contained in the prevailing harmony) must move by step. A glance at the opening bars of the first two-part Invention (quoted at example 13) will suffice to illustrate how the rule works. It will be observed here that wherever the semiquavers leap, *both* notes make good harmony with the other part; where a dissonance occurs between the two parts either one or both of them are moving by step. Not until he has fully understood this general rule should the student go on to examine the exceptions to it which Bach's music allows. These we may summarize under four headings: changing notes, octave displacement, melodic patterns, and pedals.

Changing notes and the échappée: The dissonant semiquavers marked with crosses in example 4, although proceeding by leap, are normally accepted when they occur within the so-called 'changing-note' figure, which is here shown in brackets. Two appearances of a harmony note are separated by its upper and lower auxiliary notes, one or both of which may dissonant. Changing notes are prominently used in Bach's counterpoint, usually as part of a recurring melodic figure. For other examples, the reader is referred to the fifth two-part Invention, where they appear in every single bar.

Example 4

Two-part Invention no. 3, bars 35–37

Similar to this figure is the échappée, in which a harmony note rises one step before falling a third to the next harmony note. It is found particularly at cadences and in ornamental resolution of a suspension.

Octave displacement: Unaccented semiquavers are often rendered dissonant by a procedure for which the textbooks have no name, but which may be described as 'octave displacement'. The principles governing this are best demonstrated by considering example 5(a), a pedestrian sequence which might find a place in any student exercise. What Bach himself wrote is shown in example 5(b). It will be seen that he has transferred two of the

Example 5

Two-part Invention no. 4, bars 7–11

harmony notes down an octave, in each case robbing the succeeding semi-quaver of its identity as a passing note, and so making it 'incorrect'. In a similar way a dissonance approached by the leap of a ninth is acceptable in Bach's canon if it is the result of the octave displacement of an auxiliary note (see example 6). Octave displacement is a convenient method of adjusting

Example 6

Two-part Invention no. 7, bars 17–18

the layout of the music if one part is getting a little too high or too low, but it is also important for the vitality which it can contribute to the melodic lines in general. The student should be encouraged, and not merely allowed, to imitate Bach in this way.

Melodic patterns: Bach also treated the textbook rule with license when he considered the maintenance of an established melodic phrase of greater importance than the avoidance of harmonic clashes. A look at example 7 will make this clear. Here the leaps of a third, shown by brackets, contain notes which are often at odds with the prevailing harmony; they are acceptable because they are used consistently and because the dissonances which they produce, being unaccented, are relatively mild. The entire three-

Example 7

Three-part Invention no. 6, bars 1–6

part Invention no.6 is worth looking at closely for its use of dissonance. As well as those in the example quoted there will be found other unaccented dissonances (bars 11–15 etc.) and clashes resulting from the free combination of passing and harmony notes in different voices (see especially bars 35 and 37). The guiding principle here seems to be that the logical progression of the harmony should remain undisturbed. The first of the three-part Inventions contains a *locus classicus* whose extreme dissonances the ear can accept only because the melodic lines which produce them do not individually conflict with the basic harmony at that point, which is the dominant chord of D minor (see example 8).

Example 8

Three-part Invention no. 1, bars 12–13

Pedals: Anyone familiar with the opening chorus of the *St Matthew Passion* knows how important the use of pedal points is in the construction of Bach's larger-scale works. In the slighter context of a dance movement or an Invention, however, they play a relatively small part. In the keyboard works they are often sustained by a trill, and a pedal in one voice is normally balanced by one in another voice, either immediately or in a similar passage later in the movement. They should not be overused in short pieces, but a dominant pedal is sometimes helpful in establishing a central modulation or in reinforcing the return of the home key. Naturally, any dissonant leaps arising from the use of a pedal are quite unobjectionable (see example 9), provided that the other parts themselves suggest good harmony.

Example 9

Two-part Invention no. 3, bars 5–8 (cf. bars 47–50)

Throughout this section we have continually stressed the importance of a firm harmonic framework to the design of a contrapuntal movement. Now we must consider how the harmony is to be made explicit by the combination of the various parts. In three-part work it is not usually difficult to achieve a full-sounding harmony, since three voices are sufficient to complete the chords needed, or at least to suggest them unequivocably. But in two-part writing the tussle between the desire to write interesting lines and the necessity of making the harmony complete can test the skill of even the most accomplished student.

The only harmonically 'complete' intervals in two-part writing are thirds and sixths, and it is in the interests of sonority that these intervals fall on most of the strong beats. Bach was never one to torture his part-writing to achieve this ideal, but the extent to which he observed the principle behind it is evident in even a cursory glance at any of his two-part pieces. A quick check of the first two-part Invention shows that the two voices come together on a strong beat 33 times all told, and that in all but five cases they form the interval of a third or a sixth. It is a measure of his contrapuntal skill that there is never the slightest hint that he has compromised his melodic lines to make this possible.

Of course an unvarying succession of thirds and sixths on all the strong beats in every piece would be unbearably tiresome. Fifths and octaves are freely used to begin and end a phrase, and a cadence in two-part writing, especially the final one, usually comes to rest on an octave. Accented passing notes and suspensions also provide relief from too much concord, as well as giving point and 'bite' to the rhythm. Suspensions especially are a very strong feature of Bach's style and in some instances they form the basis for an entire movement (see the two-part Invention no. 6). The student should be encouraged to study Bach's treatment of suspensions, particularly his methods of varying their resolutions, and to make good use of them in his own exercises. In doing so, he would also be well advised to heed the following two cautions:

(a) *A suspension does not necessarily mean a tie.* There exists a strong temptation in the minds of most students to tie a suspension without good reason. Whether or not a tie is advisable will largely depend upon the character of the piece, but in instrumental music it is often preferable to repeat the suspension on the strong beat for the sake of greater dissonance. The dissonance is, after all, the whole point of a suspension, and it is the alternation of discord and concord which propels the music forward. It is worth noting, however, that when the suspension is of shorter duration than its preparation Bach will usually tie it.

(b) *A tie does not necessarily mean a suspension.* The student will not go wrong here if he remembers that a suspension produces a discord. The interval of a fourth may be regarded as a dissonance in this context but the interval of a sixth may not, and a 6–5 suspension can exist only in the mind of the composer, not in the ear of the listener. There is, of course, nothing wrong with writing tied concords so long as their comparative weakness is understood and they are not used in contexts which invite a genuine suspension.

RHYTHM AND TEXTURE

The ideal contrapuntal texture of no matter what style or period seems to be that in which the various parts are, at any given moment, both melodically interdependent and rhythmically independent. In other words, counterpoint relies upon imitation and tends to avoid rhythmic sameness. All the Bach Inventions begin with a 'point' of imitation which is immediately taken up by each part in turn, and which reappears in all the voices during the course of the piece. But even in such works as the keyboard suites, where Bach is less concerned about working out the initial phrase, it is usually imitative counterpoint which carries the music along. The sharing of common musical material in this way might lead us to expect a kind of texture in which all the parts are similar in character and equal in melodic importance—just as in the history book descriptions of the Elizabethan madrigal.

In fact this is not quite so, and was never quite so in the madrigals either. Bach realized, as the madrigalists had done before him, that the bass voice plays a harmonic role quite different from that of an upper part; he knew that its freedom of movement is limited by the necessity of its defining and maintaining the basis of the harmony. In a two-part work it is usually possible for the bass to do this and match the other part in melodic interest as well. In three-part writing, however, one must be prepared to accept fairly frequent stretches of what might be called 'trio-sonata' or 'chamber-duet' texture; that is, a fairly straightforward 'continuo' bass supporting two imitative lines above. All the three-part Inventions contain examples of this kind of writing. No. 5 uses it exclusively.

Three-part writing, then, is not simply a question of adding another part to a two-strand texture. It has its own techniques and its own problems, most of which derive from the necessity of maintaining as much interest as possible in every part. Fortunately there is no need to keep all the parts active all the time, and varying the density of the texture is a virtue, not a weakness. So far as the keyboard suites are concerned, Bach is often careless of whether there are two, three, or four voices taking part, and he does not even define the absence of a part with rests. But even in the stricter counterpoint of the Inventions (and of course the fugues) he will occasionally reduce the texture to two parts for brief periods. This calls for some skill, and the student must resist the temptation to fall back on rests as a convenient and easy way out of a tight spot. A reduction in the number of voices should normally coincide with the end of a phrase, and often with a fairly well-defined cadence. The re-entry of the part, too, is something which demands considerable care. Above all, it is desirable that its reappearance should contribute something worthwhile to the music; a voice should not re-enter the texture merely because it is expedient, at a certain moment, for it to do so. For this reason it is usually advisable to accompany its re-entry with a point of imitation, using either the initial phrase of the piece or a new idea.

Example 10 has been chosen to illustrate all these points. The reader will observe a reduction in texture from three to two strands coinciding with a well-defined cadence. The alto line reappears a bar later with a point of imitation already stated in the other two parts. The passage is quite typical of Bach's methods, though it should be added that such reductions in the

Example 10

Three-part Invention no. 14, bars 14–16

texture are both brief and infrequent in short pieces like the Inventions; many of these works, in fact, keep all three parts active throughout. Reduction to a single strand, even in the two-part works, is very rare after the opening phrase. The famous octaves in the E minor fugue from the *Well-tempered Clavier*, as well as the less famous ones in the third Partita (*Burlesca*), are striking examples of a reduction in texture at points of climax or for the sake of emphasis, and recall more telling examples of the same device in other works—the third Brandenburg Concerto (opening *ritornello*), for example, and the *St Matthew Passion* ('for He hath said, I am the Son of God'). To understand the value of unison is a mark of the great contrapuntist, but it is not something with which the student need concern himself at this stage.

Even without cutting down the actual number of parts a reduction in texture is possible by a process which reverses that shown in example 2 on page 11. Bach's three-part writing is not infrequently merely a two-stranded texture in disguise. Example 11(a) shows a passage of two-part counterpoint such as Bach might well have written, and example 11(b) shows what he actually did write. It will be observed that although the texture of the second version appears to the eye much more substantial than the first, the number of notes actually sounded by the player is in each case identical.

Example 11

Three-part Invention no. 10, bars 8–11

The advantages of this technique to the student who aims to produce interesting lines in a three-part piece will be obvious.

It is in the nature of Baroque music in general that the style of a piece, or of a movement, is established in the opening bars and that a single 'affect' is maintained throughout. In longer movements we may interpret this to mean that there will be no new material introduced which conflicts, or even strongly contrasts, with the mood of the opening. In shorter pieces, such as we are concerned with here, we may take it to mean that even the rhythmic characteristics of the first bars will remain unchanged in the music which follows them. If, for example, a given opening proceeds in crotchets and quavers, the student will introduce notes of shorter value with discretion (if at all); where the opening presents an unbroken line of semi-quavers he will be wise to maintain this semiquaver movement throughout the whole piece. As a rule, the instrumental counterpoint of Bach poses no further problems of rhythmic organization. Many examination questions ask for the completion of a dance movement, and, although an opening is usually given, the student ought to acquaint himself with the rhythmic features of the dances commonly found in the Bach suites and partitas: Allemande; Courante; Sarabande; Gavotte; and Gigue.

The Inventions show little variation in rhythmic make-up in so far as they mostly maintain unbroken semiquaver movement, as indeed does a great deal of Bach's instrumental counterpoint in other works. This does not mean, of course, that any one part moves only in semiquavers, or that semiquaver movement is desirable in all parts simultaneously. Rhythmic independence is the norm, and in two-part writing this means general submission to the rule that only one part is kept busy at a time. But even this sensible caution is best discarded on occasions, and a rush of semi-quavers in *both* hands can produce a fine effect for a bar or two, particularly at moments of climax.

MUSICAL FORMS

The forms in which the student is usually asked to display his skill in Bach-style counterpoint (outside fugue and canon) are those embraced by the keyboard suites and the Inventions. These works make an admirable introduction to a study of form in Bach's music as a whole, for the principles which govern their construction (as regards both key and thematic organization) are exactly those which operate in longer works, while their relatively small dimensions make it possible to complete an entire movement as a weekend task or an examination answer.

Dance movements in binary form: Not all the movements in the Bach suites are contrapuntal but they are all useful for studying the form of his dance movements. While these are invariably binary in structure, they show sufficient diversity in the minutiae of their designs to give rise to conflicting descriptions of them in many textbooks. What our investigations should tell us is what is typical of Bach, and what is peculiar to a single movement or a few. The descriptions and analyses which follow result from a close inspection of the 120 or so dances in Bach's principal works for solo clavier—the English and French Suites, the Partitas, and the 'Forty-eight'.

Except for the preludes, the movements of the Baroque suite usually follow the traditional dance form of the period, which consists of two complementary sections, each of them played twice. The first begins in the tonic and closes in a related key; the second leads back to the original key, usually encompassing other modulations *en route*. The music of each section is materially the same, but the second part is usually longer than the first (and *never* shorter), because there are more keys to be included and because of the need to re-establish the tonic at the end. An analysis of all the binary movements in the works mentioned shows us that the most favoured single proportion is one of exactly equal length in each section. However, the other proportions used together outnumbered this one by about three to one. The following table shows how many examples of the various possibilities exist in the works analysed. However, there is no need for the student to be aware of these details when attempting dance forms in the Bach style. What is important is to realize that a feeling for proportion and balance

Number of bars in each part expressed as a ratio	*Number of examples in the works analysed*
1 : 1	31 (26 per cent)
1 : 2	26 (22 per cent)
3 : 4	14 (12 per cent)
2 : 3	10 (8 per cent)
4 : 5	6
1 : 3	6
3 : 5	2
2 : 5	2
Others	23 (one example of each)

Total: 120

in such movements is very strong, and the above table clearly shows a preference for the simpler ratios. All the movements of Bach's suites except the preludes derive from music originally intended to accompany the formal steps of the dances from which they take their names. Balance and symmetry of design were necessary to allow the dancers to complete their figures and to avoid wrong-footing them. The movements of Bach's keyboard suites were not, of course, designed to accompany dancing, and the original dance-types have become highly stylized. Nevertheless, they show their derivations not only in tempo and rhythmic characteristics but also in the neat proportions of their structures.

The number of bars in each section will largely depend upon the speed of the movement and the time signature. The gigues are usually the longest; that in the fifth English Suite, for example (in $\frac{3}{8}$ time), has no fewer than forty-eight bars of music in each section. The Allemande in the third Partita, on the other hand, is by no means the only movement with only sixteen bars altogether. One can only offer generalities, but it is worth noting that most of the binary movements with common time signatures, such as $\frac{4}{4}$, $\frac{3}{4}$, $\frac{6}{8}$, $\frac{9}{8}$, and so on, contain between eight and sixteen bars in the first section and between twelve and thirty-two bars in the second. By far the commonest aggregate is $8 + 16$ bars, and while there is no need for the student to restrict his own solutions to these dimensions, they do provide a serviceable framework for his first attempts.

Perhaps the most important thing to learn from this analysis is that each section of a binary movement, whatever its length, should include an even number of bars. The dance movements which total an uneven number are sufficiently rare to be ignored. This is not just a question of adding up at the end to see if the double bar line has come at the right place. The student must be aware of the length and balance of his phrases, and, if the dance has been conceived in this way, an uneven number of bars will not be merely numerically odd—they will sound 'odd'. Bach's music is by no means always 'square' like this, and only about half of the Inventions total an even number of bars. The dances are exceptional, and the reasons for their symmetry I have already summarized.

Key and tonal relationships (one of the great discoveries of the Baroque period) form the basis of the binary structure in Bach's suites and demand a good deal of forethought. As we stressed earlier, a sense of direction in the counterpoint can come only from the harmony, and a sense of direction in the harmony (as in hiking) depends upon a clear idea of the destination, and (it might be added) at least a rough idea of the expected time of arrival. A map is also tremendously helpful, and this is available if we take the trouble to study the paths which Bach's music has taken.

There are always at least two keys, and normally three, which form the harmonic framework of a dance movement. The piece naturally begins and ends in the tonic; a closely related key is reached at the end of the first part, and usually another related key somewhere towards the middle of the second section. In major keys the central modulation (at the double bar) is almost invariably to the dominant, the only exceptions being a few cases where the music comes to rest *on* the dominant of the home key. The cadence at this point very often 'rhymes' with the final cadence of the piece in the way shown in example 12. The second section, usually longer than the first, passes through a wide range of keys, but there is nearly always one modulation (and sometimes more than one) which stands out from the others because it is established with a formal cadence. Often, it too 'rhymes' with the final cadence (see again example 12), but in any case its structural importance is unmistakable. The key most commonly reached at this point is the relative minor, but the supertonic minor is also frequently found.

Example 12

English Suite no.2: Gigue ('rhyming' cadences)

(a) bars 32–34

(b) bars 58–60

(c) bars 72–74

From these observations, it is possible to sketch the tonal outlines of a major-key dance movement in the following way:

$$\|: I - V :\|: (V) - VI \text{ minor} - I :\|$$
(or II minor)

Some examples of the first type are the Gavotte, Air, and Gigue in the fourth French Suite, the Minuet I in the first Partita, and the Courante in the fifth Partita. With the alternative modulation to the subdominant minor may be cited the Bourrées from the French Suite no. 6 and the English Suite no. 1. These movements should be studied if possible, and the student should look out for more examples in other works.

These keys perform a structural function—they form the pillars which support the tonal superstructure of the movement. Other keys will also be used, of course. The central cadence (V) might be approached by way of the relative minor, and there will certainly be other modulations in the second section. Towards the end there is often a swerve towards the sub-dominant key which acts as a kind of brake on the harmony, not to be confused with the flattened seventh which Bach often introduces in the opening bars without modulation. (Mozart, too, was very fond of this harmonic twist at the beginning of a composition.) Subsidiary modulations after the double bar often result from the use of sequence, and it would be both foolish and unnecessary to attempt to formulate rules for them here. The student can safely be left to investigate Bach's methods for himself, but it is worth reminding him that the wider his range of modulation the more care he must take over re-establishing the main tonality. Where Bach has written a long piece passing through many keys, we often find a few bars of dominant preparation (perhaps with a dominant pedal) before the tonic returns; frequently, too, its return is emphasized by reference to the melodic figure which opened the piece.

So far we have been concerned only with major keys. Minor keys provide a greater choice of central modulation, and therefore of key structure as a whole, and the student should take as his models (at least to begin with) those schemes most favoured by Bach himself. These are as follows:

(a) $\|: \ \mathrm{I} - \mathrm{V(minor)} \ :\|: \ \mathrm{(V\ minor)} - \mathrm{IV\ minor} - \mathrm{I} \ :\|$

(b) $\|: \ \mathrm{I} - \mathrm{III(major)} \ :\|: \ \mathrm{(III\ major)} - \mathrm{V\ minor} - \mathrm{I} \ :\|$

(or IV minor)

(c) $\|: \mathrm{I} - \mathrm{I(dominant)} \ :\|: \ \mathrm{(I\ dom)} - \mathrm{III\ major} - \mathrm{I} \ :\|$

The following examples should be studied with reference to the above outlines: (a) Courante from the second French Suite and Burlesca from the third Partita; (b) Air from the French Suite no. 2, Gavotte I from the third English Suite, and Minuet from the second French Suite; (c) Minuet II from the French Suite no. 3, and Courante from the third Partita.

A few points are worth making here. Except in those movements (group (c)) where the first section ends *on* the dominant without modulation, it is rare for Bach to establish the relative major after the double bar. A middle cadence in the dominant minor (V minor) always comes to rest upon a major chord or upon a unison, and so prepares for the repeat of the first section. The final chord of a minor piece, however, is much more commonly minor (or a unison), although in about 25 per cent of the dance movements Bach closes with a 'picardy' third. As in major-key pieces, transitory modulations play an important part, and here again the student should look closely at Bach's methods in the examples mentioned and elsewhere.

A carefully planned harmonic scheme is more than usually necessary in movements which do not rely upon the opening figure for their melodic material. Only in the gigues is Bach concerned with developing the material in fugal fashion, although imitative openings are common in other dances too, even when the first figure is harmonized. After the opening theme has been stated and the tonic key established, the music proceeds towards the central cadence by the extension of figures, either new or detached from the principal tune. Sequence and invertible counterpoint are the commonest ways of carrying these figures forward and developing them. The second section usually begins with material similar to the opening, perhaps with the first tune inverted or with the material interchanged between the hands. After a cadence in a new key (often occurring at the eighth bar or thereabouts) there might follow some fresh material not heard before the double bar, leading the music back to the tonic key, where the piece will end with a cadential phrase similar to that which concluded the first section.

Needless to say, this outline will not hold good for all the Bach dance movements; it may, indeed, apply to very few of them. It is important, though, that the student should have some such plan in mind before he puts pen to paper, even if the music he eventually writes leads him in other directions. The gigues, and occasionally other dances too, rely more for their material upon the opening theme, but binary movements in general depend as much upon invention as upon resource, making their effect by graceful ideas, nicely-balanced phrases, and a well-defined and satisfying harmonic framework.

Inventions: Much of what has been said about dance movements in Bach's suites applies also to the composition of Inventions. Unlike the dances, however, these works are always concerned with searching out the contrapuntal possibilities of their opening melodic figures. Bach designed them as a training ground where, to quote his own words again, 'those desirous of learning are shown . . . not alone to have good ideas (*inventiones*), but *to develop the same well*'. An Invention grows out of its initial idea, and so that we may be clearly aware of the identity of this idea it is often stated unaccompanied, as in a fugue. In fact, some of the three-part Inventions (those in D major and A major for example) are hardly distinguishable from genuine fugues, while the F minor Invention, with its chromatic subject and its triple counterpoint, shows a degree of resource not often paralleled even in the 'Forty-eight'. There are two-part Inventions as well, such as the one in E flat major, in which not a scrap of new melodic material is introduced after the first three or four bars. Such works are distinguished from fugues mainly by their brevity, which often results from the brevity of the opening 'subject' itself; and they usually dispense with the more cerebral devices of fugal writing, such as augmentation, diminution, and stretto. Inversion, however, is not uncommon.

Fugue is not, strictly speaking, a form, and there are episodic Inventions just as there are episodic fugues. But even those Inventions furthest removed from fugue lean heavily upon their initial thematic material. The first of the two-part Inventions, for example, might well impress the listener as a rather merry piece of ingenuous counterpoint, in which the composer has been at no pains to parade his command of fugal resource. Analysis reveals its outstanding ingenuity, however, by showing how the entire piece is built from the initial phrase (x) or its inversion (see example 13).

Example 13

Two-part Invention no. 1, bars 1–4

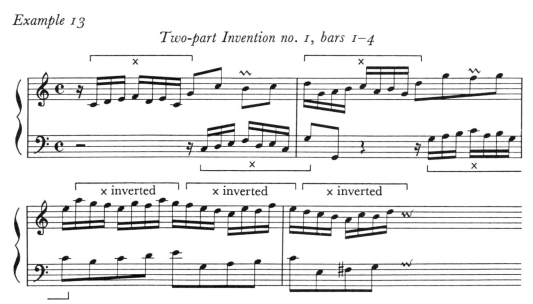

Some of the Inventions rely more upon the introduction of new material than others. The kind of treatment the student chooses to adopt will depend partly upon the character of the opening and partly upon his own ability to recognize and develop its characteristics. When to fall back upon the given material and when to invent new ideas are problems which test the instinct of the composer as much as his knowledge of the models. The only piece of advice one can offer the beginner here is the reminder that the more episodic (or improvisatory) the music, the greater its need for a firm harmonic basis.

Common to all the Inventions, however, is the imitative opening. In the two-part Inventions the intial phrase may be announced alone (see example 13), in which case the upper voice invariably begins, or the two parts may start together. In either case the initial figure of the right hand is immediately echoed in the left, usually at the octave (see again example 13), but sometimes in the dominant key, as in a fugue. The three-part Inventions usually announce the first theme in descending order of voices (S–A–B), and present a quasi-fugal exposition with the second voice entering at the dominant pitch. Contrary to fugal practice, however, the theme is never announced alone in the three-part Inventions, but always with a bass which itself usually contributes to the melodic material of the piece.

After the opening subject has been stated in all the parts, the Inventions proceed in much the same way as the contrapuntal dances described above, except that there is greater reliance upon the opening theme, less insistence upon two- and four-bar phrases, and no repeats. (The two-part Invention no. 6 is an exception to this last remark, and the only Invention in binary form.) Except for those which most nearly approach the character of a ricercare, the Inventions, like the dances, tend to build their harmonic framework around three main key-centres which are established by well-defined, often 'rhyming' cadences. The first of these corresponds with the double-bar cadence in a binary-form movement, and usually occurs about one-third of the way through. What follows it is usually an interchange of ideas between the hands, leading to another cadence in a related key, after which the music finds its way back to the tonic. The choice of keys for these main modulations follows fairly closely the schemes put forward for the dance movements on pages 28 and 29.

So far as the constructional details of the Inventions are concerned, one can offer no more precise rules than in the case of binary-form dances, and this, perhaps, is one reason why they provide such fruitful material for study. In each case the challenge is the same: to supply the best possible working-out of the given material. But the solution in each case is arrived at differently because the material is different, and one kind of treatment will not suit all kinds of theme. Each Invention tests the student anew in a way which demands more than mere facility in counterpoint. Given intelligent study, the Inventions of Bach can indeed provide a 'strong foretaste of composition'.

EXERCISES

THE exercises which follow are intended for performance on a keyboard instrument (harpsichord or clavichord), but there is no reason why some of them at least should not be worked in other media at the discretion of the tutor. Bach and his contemporaries rarely phrased their music, but it is always capable of being phrased. The student should not regard his work as complete until it shows indications of phrasing, speed, and dynamics, without, however, any of the fussy detail which mars so many modern editions of Baroque music.

1. Complete the right-hand part of the following minuet. The quaver movement should be maintained for most of the movement.

Bach. French Suite no. 2

2. Complete the following Courante by continuing the right-hand part as far as the double bar, and the left-hand part from the double bar to the end. Melodic figures used in the first section should reappear in the second.

Bach. Partita no. 5

34

3. Add to the right-hand part a bass. Then complete the Courante with a second section of sixteen bars, including a cadence in E minor at the eighth bar. The last four bars should echo those of the first section.

Bach. French Suite no. 5

4. Add a bass line to the following, and then complete the Bourrée with a second section slightly longer than the first.

Bach. English Suite no. 1

5. Continue the following opening to complete a binary movement about forty bars long. Finish the first section with a cadence in B flat major, and include a well-defined modulation to C minor fairly early in the second part.

Handel. Suite no. 7

6. Without attempting continuous three-part counterpoint, finish the following Gavotte. The first section should be eight bars long, ending in D major; the second section should be twice that length, establishing the key of E minor at its eighth bar. Aim above all for grace and symmetry, but let the bass take an active part.

Bach. French Suite no. 5

7. Complete the following Allemande:

J. C. Richter

8. Complete the following Allemande:

Handel. Suite no. 16 (transposed)

9. Add a bass line to the following, and then continue both parts to complete an Invention about forty bars in length.

Bach. Two-part Invention no. 4

10. Continue the following to make a two-part Invention of about twenty to twenty-four bars.

Bach. English Suite no. 4

11. Complete the following Prelude in two parts:

Purcell. Suite no. 5

12. Complete the following three-part Invention:

J. S. Bach

13. Complete the following three-part Invention:

Bach. Three-part Invention no. 8

14. Complete the following Prelude in three parts:

J. S. Bach